UNANIMAL, COUNTERFEIT, SCURRILOUS

Also by Mark Anthony Cayanan

Narcissus
Except you enthrall me

MARK ANTHONY CAYANAN

UNANIMAL, COUNTERFEIT, SCURRILOUS

NEW POEMS

First published 2021
from the Writing and Society Research Centre
at Western Sydney University
by the Giramondo Publishing Company
PO Box 752
Artarmon NSW 1570 Australia
www.giramondopublishing.com

Designed by Jenny Grigg
Typeset by Andrew Davies
in 9/15 pt Tiempos Regular

Cover image: François Andriot
Boy removing a thorn from his foot (fl. 1655–1660?)
© Royal Academy of Arts, London

Printed and bound by Ligare Book Printers
Distributed in Australia by NewSouth Books

A catalogue record for this book is available from the
National Library of Australia.

ISBN: 978-1-925818-69-7

The Giramondo Publishing Company acknowledges the support
of Western Sydney University in the implementation of its book
publishing program.

This project has been assisted by the Commonwealth Government
through the Australia Council, its arts funding and advisory body.

I'm not the starlet I thought I was.
Frank O'Hara

Contents

1

No unusual difficulty was involved; instead, he was being paralysed by a scruple born of aversion.

As Aschenbach

This isn't about how, whatever it is, sour and stale, it pushes against the shut mouth of self-refusal. Something that ought to happen keeps almost happening, mornings happen, and rain tries the window, through the window is a room of windows, the room, when it moves, moves like a chain-link fence. Every recent hour is dead, and the body, which pretends that decay's a fair price for wisdom, nevertheless concedes to the details of its life. But quietly. In truth, when life happens, it happens in the fourth person. In truth, no warning shot was fired, in the walls of corrugated metal are bullet holes through which futures have escaped, and when asked about him, she takes his young face out of a shoe box and reconstitutes her rage. The fourth person permits one to sentimentalise the pain of others without the shamelessness of co-optation. The body must find another body, sometimes this body is its own. Despite itself, the body hopes to resist the story it inexorably becomes, because the undiscardable body's the joke that needs to be explained, let the needing wait.

Wind and teeth

The boat through green water enters a dead god's calcified breath. His gasp when he flicks on the light of his hard hat is a door for his body, which, moving, keeps constituting new frailties. The cave preserves the dark, scatters it in small rooms. Some doorless rooms remain unopened. Unlike the wind that nudges the boat farther inward, his body just another guest, his persistence is a kind of grace that allows him to make the inevitable

meaningful. The rowing takes over an hour, he overhears the winged murmurs of bats and grows tired of looking at stalactites with his mouth closed, the oars demand an endurance he thinks he used to possess. Sensing his quiet, the guide tells him to turn off the torch, and the dark makes them indistinguishable from the cave's secrets. He knows his disappeared body exists by his fear, only another god can force both secrets open. The guide, who earns a living by eliciting awe out of these mysteries, stops at a bank that leads to another grotto. In his awe

he is prosaic, he examines the drawings on a wall, charcoaled by families who hid from the war. Their boredom crawls towards posterity, history is its own unyielding force, consumes them, here with no one to make time answer for the grief it authorises, is it time or grief that becomes trivia. When he picks up stones and lays them flat on a rock, he turns them into eyes, nose, a sad mouth, a sharper tongue. Muddy light makeshifts the face. He washes his hands in the river, under the surface the cold leads to more chambers, some as beautiful as a young body. The guide takes him

down a path where ladders resting between boulders are bridges. The body's route is reticence, legs trying to scramble nimbly past the no of inconsistent limestones. The body shimmying between longing and anger. The body clutches a rope and fights the current to get across the river. The guide, while waiting for the body to catch its breath, smokes a cigarette, a man without a government. The body knows what its frailties are useful for. Before the guide asks if they're ready to descend deeper

already this body that wants to be wind and teeth, the body that wants to be noticed, has prepared its lie. Making do with a language neither of them owns, he enters the great void of his middle age expecting profound transformation.

Variations on the word 'pass'

As when something despite itself gives in to another. After he survived bullets from the first attempt, his luck runs out once they brandish cleavers. They stash verdigris-covered coins with unreadable characters in the town hall basement, turn the museum into a fast food joint. Counter wiped clean of instant broth and grease. Or when out of a flute glass, a dust jacket, and the hangover he hasn't slept off, he handcrafts a disposable stiletto. When a dog barks, the dog barks ominously.

As when hose-faced he ambles into the library of politically sketchy atlases but, after finding himself in the transcript of a stranger's dreams, walks out. Righteousness restored, antlered body unprepared for either scorn or, worse, nonchalance, and between one unrehearsed emotion and another there lies a third, which, were he to detect it, would ruin the parable. Upon seeing parts of her son, the mass grave intricate as a honeycomb, the clear-eyed mother insists on trimming his fingernails.

As when the sky borrows the colour of October, sombre rooms hanging in the air. Their shadows trail along the roof as they check which of the orange tiles they could pry free with a hammer claw. Shadows, unsinister and not, impair everyone. The wind waits, as the wind does, as assailants do, they wear masks and fade into the night like sirens. Shirt too tight around his waist, he thinks of how beauty, once the most negligible thing about himself, is the one loss he's managed to invent great memories of.

As when they prowl the unlit alleys like the petty criminals whose lives they've handled, they say there are those who live in the roots of trees. When it rains, they hang from the underside of leaves, and when something a little more substantial than a knowing look is exchanged between them. Days later she remembers the smell of shit on her son's body. A man who doesn't ask for permission goes blind the next day, an awful echoing noise that the audience overhears.

As when he turns his shirt inside out and looks to the sky for affirmation. A neighbour feeds his children prawn crackers while his mother talks to a journalist. The children are used to seeing her in tears and so don't turn their heads. They remove the cardboard and know it's him through the thorny heart on his forearm. She unrolls a high-school diploma, they preserve her grief in pictures. As when his life is on a list of casualties in a notebook, her sleeping head flattening the spring. This sinking city.

Wonders and terrors of the variegated earth

While they play cards someone strums a few chords and they supply the plaintive voice, supply the baby screaming in a corner, the husband humming as he pees on a fence,

the tourists memorialising the show with their phones. They use the word slums and make the evening more important. Having flown in from a continent that's never regretted its vanity, they've put themselves in good humour by buying this city's flea-market linen. Too happy, their happiness the colour of cholera, they tire quickly of haggling

with hawkers. A mock summer has set in and since the typhoon which will kill several of them is still half a sea away, they hop from one bus onto another, feet grey-black, hands smelling of garlic and vinegar.

He was most surprisingly conscious of an odd expansion within himself, a kind of roving unrest, a youthfully ardent desire for faraway places, a feeling so intense, so new or at least unaccustomed and forgotten for so long, that he stopped short as if rooted to the spot

As final in form as a seizure, this longing he wants to sacrifice a name to: in this humid heat it deflates like a body after orgasm, at his age it's a front-end loader backing into a street, everyone walking around it in hurried steps:

its goal is omnipresence:

its source, whose inattentive erection is a summary of his life, summons a look that has the eloquence of a dormant volcano: there's rainwater in that look,

like a pig it roots into dirt for fungi: once he overheard his mother say that his father smelled of cigarettes and embarrassment: he inherits from him the kind of look that's also an appeal for pardon, says

oops: the dream's only expectedly erotic: a post-winter vineyard under a sky with a blue that burns and clouds that curl like sighs: maybe he wants his longing inhaled, maybe inside a mouth, wants it with notes of apple blossom and cherry: to demonstrate he pops

his lips the way a drag queen would: he loves his ephemera the way a house cat sharpens her claws on the couch, meaning

constantly he's been carrying the look within him: when he fishes it from his left lung and opens it, out unrolls an ocean: in it are trenches that swallow saltwater, ugly fish call it their home, and mermen with dull tails braid each other's hair in the steady dark: their eyes when they blink light up the opal walls like a disco:

he rides a vaporetto across his ocean until he reaches the canals, bisected every which way by alleys that reek of spunk and unaffordable healthcare:

its pigeon population condescends to the tourists posing at the square and aren't its altars enamel and gold: when he finishes a manuscript of socially acceptable self-deceptions, he picks

his life off

the shit-smeared masegno pavement and wears it like a backpack stuffed with newspaper, every word's a rejection:

turning to those who shrill in bougie tones that locals dismiss as an ambient burden, won't you tell them how you make this city sputter and smart from the tiny desires it contrives and keeps thwarting: in your bawdy city

tenderness, priceless as a knock-off murano, marvellous as red wine, claims his best elegies and kisses:

He could no longer dismiss as mere fancy his fear

He's reduced to prayers whenever he inspects his
hairline he knows who he is he's remained the same
minor affliction his past
                has whittled him down to some days are
better than others he writes home about his faith and
walks along the river because he hopes he's someone
                whose thoughts need sorting out he waits
behind a door plots a genealogy that's yet to exist
snail-mails past lovers thank-you
                notes written on lavender paper so they
don't regret times he's dropped by drunk to the point
of vulnerability the degree of lonely
                that needs to wind its fingers around
another's hair it could've been the beginning of
unvanquishable affection they could've been
                anybody he breathes in the night and what
does it smell of now that it's one in a litany of nights
that never lead to the one thing he stops
                himself from over-investing in his online
displays of self-pity by taking to the road a voyeuristic
thrillseeker the country's gone to shit but
                he's convinced he's protected by being
too often alone when he's bored as he often is he has
enemies lurking under convenience-store
                canopies they must be harmed before they
make him he makes him he ribbons his concerns
around a jalousie, distressed ends

dangling outside his bedroom and
entertains himself by waiting for the suitor who shall
win his evening race every evening's erased his words
mean little to him after he's said them he
cultivates lives in case he's no longer anything worth
living for as much as when he first felt
alive within him is no game low-stakes
enough
afoot long enough.

Motus animi continuus

Of course he loves this servitude, the want, the wishing it away

takes along a needle, when his date leaves the table for a minute, drops blood from the pricked finger into the red wine, admits to this the next day. One must be calm, follow to the end this novelistic logic at the expense of survival

half his body in the drying cement. They've asked him to sing carols to keep him awake

In the privacy of his bathroom he takes off his dentures, the part that makes him human

not a relic of the past or raffish flirtation but a trap for fools: to say things little by little, to merely relent

early dictionaries house different species of mosquitoes and the six types of fever: daily, tertian, imagined, weak and prolonged, desirous, and severe and incensed

He inhabits the rage of a white man who, white rage over-brimmed, doesn't know how it feels to be second-guessed

collects the photographs in an album: unmade bed, viscous streak on the vanity, ashtrays crammed with anxiety, everything that deserves photography. Days devoted, at intervals of hours, to following the changes of shadow and blight

the rolling landscape with its reliable winter rains and photogenic summers, the name recalling musket fire and viticulture

With a glass to his lips he indulges in light gossip, the sort that begets ruin. When he leans back on his chair

provocateur, who pours wrath into the wrong cup, puts climax before penetration. This afternoon shame crawls down a wall like the setting sun

the residents sleep on the street, aftershocks continuing well past midnight, the second floor of the apartment resting on a man's broken back. Four hours with no hope of rescue, the gurgling from his lungs quiets

He spends his most vital years denying the value of revelation, holding with both hands a bouquet of mirrors

the tongue that says, This tastes good, but whose natural modesty forbids it to say more: all other declarations are polysyllabic mysteries on the plastic wrapper

only sugar mills, none worth more than a few pesos. When they're drafted to work in gold mines thousands die, unable to farm and forced to live on palms and bananas

When they open fire he runs through the plaza and hides in the cubicle of a women's comfort room; the government however grants them omniscience

to realise the plan they bludgeon him, stuff the body into a culvert, noisy miners flying in and out of the field. Then return to their homes

the windiest months, soil frozen from December through most of March

He wears bermudas and sandals, will play nice if they can only prove they're on his side. He'll bring them, brothers, back to their families, give them a box of vitamins

the revolution of language isn't for the prose but for the writer—prose in nylons and lace-fronts and from falsies

from lusty fern clusters, misshapen trees with hairy branches that shoot flowers milky as semen; between the knotty stalks of bamboo the eyes of a tiger sparkle, a dream spores

He knows just when to press the wounds so they prove inspirational enough, can fester before the hypothetical audience

o cautery that heals, o consummating hand, o touch so fine it satisfies eternity. The lamps of burning fire, o deaths out of life

they gut a pig, snap a chicken's neck, burn the entrails, perform an exorcism, anything to ward off evil: amulet, rice in a cone, red carpet, chain letter, envelopes with sloppy calligraphy

An exaggerated shrug to go with his bewildered expression, as if to ask Who, me, he wears skirts, codpieces, and breasts, all made from the city's nightly debris

a little sleep, locked together, for an interval. Let the evening mount. Let him ride

both grander and stranger than someone new can imagine, the graffiti roaring into beauty when the train homes into a station, passengers alert as startled birds. They've kept the windows open to give the illusion of life without commitment

He hopes, out of his cowardice, for the best: to be the great betrayer. Hearing bits of human voices streaming down the drainpipe—always the belief in being gracious—he slams the window shut

madness being fashionable at the moment: a foul-mouthed dictator and his actors recreate an asylum before a national theatre

on train tracks, in front of an all-girls' school, across bed-bugged mattresses and rattan settees, through their fingers a man sprawled on the sidewalk, here's one last glance:

2

He had been young and raw when the era was young and raw.

As Aschenbach

1

Who setting out to voyage must have imagined which shores to avoid, get out.

Whose violence to himself when he turns away from any man or moves towards him with ill-disguised tenderness is, though enjoyed, denied, whose diaristic writings speak of being safely overwhelmed by pleasure. Whose scenarios of unsanctioned passion are swaths of an inner life repurposed from bourgeois melodrama, hands slightly reptilian and daily a proxy for knowing.

Who, years past ripe, gapes open, whose nearness to ruin adds an occasional beauty, discernible only when bent down, nape exposed. Shorter than average height, clean-shaven, whose head is still too large for his once-dainty body, hair brushed back, thinning at the crown.

1

Whose method of dealing with the boredom of outgrowing libertinism and adopting the courtliness of solitude is self-mockery. His is either a well-oiled universe or a chaos huddled together, still he's a mannish character, unanimal, counterfeit, scurrilous.

Who freely divulges the secrets of those he feels no loyalty to,

whose moral determination bypasses learning, thus feeding his wish to be telegenically evil. Who slingshoots profanities at the incorruptible priest with his god's stigmata, only to tremble down to the ground in repentance, how brightly does sorry aureole his body. Sweaty, envious of the dogged crowd, who mislabels his own caprices, so on-brand, as childlike profundity.

1

Whose technique consists of flashing eyes, an ingratiating grin, and a barrage of unwelcome questions. How frequently do you follow yourself. Why do you not share.

Who pours cold water on himself, shrieking as he does, and faces forward, but with some show of modesty that used to be nearly provocative. Who watches through his fingers the heroes of his age come and go, Mahler's Fifth Symphony, redundant as an overcast sky.

Whose timidity masks the mundane ugliness proper to all who, after a history of rejection, convert their desire to be stripped of yearning into a source of authority. Who nurses a cocktail as everybody else builds their dioramas of suffering, who grows in and out of a deception.

Naïve and sentimental

Take the cotton gown off and see his back covered in summer
evenings, moles glistening like sinister stars, penis so
stage-frightened it curls
into a disclaimer. His face carries a clock's alarm, it would
all soon be over,
don't be stupid, you know it won't.
Outside the hospital: an ordinary parking lot where cars
drive out to an ordinary Wednesday; in his room: the
frustrating lack of progress bloats out to every corner
until you find you
shouldn't breathe. Because you want to, you inhale the
sweat off his standard pillow, a river whose breakers
are planks of treated wood, enough self-preservation
to make you wonder
who you're there as, etc.
Around his neck, tied to an invisible chain, is an invisible
key, off-silver as a tooth jacket, which because no
one's looking can open his breast—dig
past the rib cage right down to his spongy lungs until you're
led to the most gorgeous garden: wax flowers, golden
wattles, hay fever, and royal bluebells.
You're the kind of person who'd think it's world-sickness,
this parasitic exchange of maladies, which isn't
as complex as it sounds, is it nothing but itchy skin, there
where his fear wants out. When he shows off the scabbed-over
cuts and you don't

touch him as a way of proving to yourself your worth, there's
a vulgar pettiness to this crucial display of reserve,
also a nobility that arises from the decision
to be exposed as ugly,
which in fact is what one of you is, how are you changing,
just by the fact of each other's presence?

Naïve and sentimental

Back when he rode shotgun was when his beauty gave him balls, wanted an answer fitted into his mouth, rode shotgun and entertained the romance of oblivion, a road trip with no return, one wild strawberry sunset after another and roadside cafes sold the best milkshakes and you couldn't help but know his hand every hour even when you kept your eyes duty-straight, your eyes already red, him halving the dusky silence, Let's make a stop, to which, coy, you'd go, For what, a neon motel magically appearing, its sheets crisp, and he half-listened to your secret noises as you slept, a sitcom with a laugh track to keep him company, you never having this dream because it wasn't yours, him swallowing the dream every time it wanted to buzz out of his mouth like flesh flies breeding in his stomach, greed in their honest wings, dearest for whom you vault over the limits of convincing fantasy, you could've been tired for as long as you wanted and he could've spent the rest of his life devising ways to unfasten the night from time, but instead he intended to suffer quietly because it was safer that way, he recycled sunsets while you spun omens of catastrophe from all his showy silences, flies erupting from his ear canals, on days when you turned to him as if you could want how he wants, adept at preemptive apologies and not much in you to be a menace to yourself, haven't you borrowed his sins enough to prove you were young once, and true, and no one else was in on it, the neon motel reappearing like a promise, but then when you didn't

One among

27A seasoned backpacker kept asking for gin and ginger
ale from
flight attendant who during a stopover hires a catamaran
for the day to go snorkelling
34C livid when she can't give him his whisky on the rocks
with no ice who upon entering a cab that smells of
grease and farts cracks open a window with the
depth of resentment that often accompanies a sense
of entitlement
driver snickering as
midnight DJ harangues
newly single caller the streets have evened out into oiled
anonymity he takes his dead heart with him to work
and in line for the train overhears
government clerk gossiping with an office mate about her
younger sibling a performance artist who on stage used
to snap pigeons' necks they've since quit their
imagination unfortunately limited to borrowing
feats of depravity which at this point in history have
ceased being so novel now they're one of
1.6 million of their kind in the country working five days a
week 11 hours a day they sweat shallots and ginger
in a pot that spans two burners adds among other
death sentences two pounds of butter the invitation
to hunger wafts across the street towards a bank with
security guard with no record of aggressive behaviour until
six years later will hold a gun to his wife's temple

five straight days without sleep can make anyone
unforgiving but today
promodiser wife applies highlighting powder to a customer's
cheeks using an angled brush that's more than her
daily wage she hums a song from the jeepney as little
by little she's turned further away from herself
everyone dropping time in spendthrift ways
she isn't a customer just a working student with enough
motivation though lacking direction the Ultra
Lotto jackpot will hit P1.18 billion she'll spend her
allowance on tickets the body once mastered must
have no need for food she bums cigarettes off her
sophomore best friend his phone constantly vibrating
in comp class just wanting the one thing grows
impatient with those who refuse to send dick pics
no danger more common than a predatory body he
sneaks love into the chat it's an easy bribe

Sentence with charming composure in the empty and severe service of form

Years before he admits to an audience of none how many of his ex post facto epiphanies are bullshit, he thought, They could only love each other within the limits of their hunger, beyond which love is anaemic as memory, the kind that seems noble and inspires slight embarrassment.

No longer was he young and raw though the error remained young and raw

Dearest little unfinishable selves, look
at your lone body and how it can't outgrow
its reticence, cowled souls bold enough to play
coy but with a Rilkean swagger owned only
by those expert at being separate, outside
in the smog of all your indisposed cities, daybreak
is its known sounds, cranes undo what
apostlebirds call, autumn trees not yet denuded
not angry, stillborn versions, every one of you
misleading and wildly desirable, the bone wall
disappears each hour's promise into the commonplace
with you this default self shares no history
except the keening he makes and can you repair
his faith, not built to wait, for whom he waits, he waits

Essays on transformation

You wade through flood to get from one end of the city to your apartment, detritus floating around your thighs. Once the power's restored, you watch the news for an updated death toll and, as a tourist understands kinship, in earnest you consume replicable griefs.

≈

From soot-covered cities making unsacred noises when against one another bang minor gods and sweaty bears and turnstiles and sodomy, the fable: rat, quick caught in glue, flypaper.

≈

In this transformation-facsimile, the hero hasn't sweated the dye off his imperial and invisible bits of death don't quite yet hang in the sultry air.

≈

In your despair, a respectable amount of preening. The overnight bus makes a stop at that forgettable town where foreign miners worked a mountain until its face collapsed, trees piled up in a ravine. For the preening in your despair, despair.

≈

Beware of bone-tiredness when it leads to decision-making. Even if the sky were a sullied blue and made of wool, enjoy some light beer. Nobody lives anew.

≈

If the neighbours nod towards the house of the men who put a grocery bag over his head and dragged him away, his body found the next morning in a vacant lot, Jesus, retreat back into distraction.

≈

Given the universal truth that it's better to be thought of as nasty and therefore alone than alone because ugly, you make a small show of peeing in the community pool. Given that the only place in which ideas about the world are as horrible as their fruition is the world, swinging between sin and sinner, the resentment you redirect towards those unburdened with guilt endures and nourishes.

≈

If awe and death don't work, the general says, then maybe declaring the war's been won would. Where justice is a long con, there's collective fervour. Yours makes the racket of smaller wings.

≈

When they live in each other for an hour, the poet says, their reasons unpublic, they have a park for that. No society doesn't regulate it. Here where there are too many malls and no parks, the third-floor toilet will do, the specific rows of a movie house, if done often enough it's only as dishonourable as picking your nose, late night and careless in the back of a bus.

≈

If given a choice between postponing your kind's anger because there are revolutions more important and freestyling to your hunger as around you everything's at 900°, here's another bucket.

That's no symbol, that's a fucking stretch mark. Whose call would you trust, no tyranny more democratic than detachment.

♒

Because you suspect it's cowardice, it's cowardice.

Is there more to your cowardice. This wreath of impatiens, yours. No.

♒

Or, having in your childhood suffocated under the weight of being shamed, you had killed the way you gestured with your hands, killed the way you thought, in the bathroom you rehearsed your voice until it bounced off the tiles in the expected manner, you thought but thought in secret, killed it, how expertly you could pick up a stone. You join the throng, from it emerges the solidarity your desires had once deprived you of, and throw the stone.

♒

If all the casual katabatic trips haven't made a man out of you, then be another man.

3

Now he had to keep on wanting what he wanted yesterday.

As Aschenbach

There's no knowing now, knowing dignity's no longer a reason to keep to a life that precludes abandon. Uneventful afternoons, every same old doubt gets reinvented: doubt's the dependable coat you head out with in the crisp morning, there's no crisis you can't walk away from, dailiness sluices down the borrowed skin. Bite an occasional random bullet and sneeze out shrapnel, hum love songs to a waterless urinal, you can't hold wine the way your body used to. Eyes quick to dull, you can always eavesdrop on what can't ever be regained, you shouldn't leer at ghosts just because they've no shame, who when you speak would be willing to listen. At which point did your life become a checklist of easy hungers. It's OK, you've grieved enough, asked to see the holes in his palms enough, when you lick your mouth in a suggestive fashion you only look ridiculous. Now's when you replace dignity with another species of fear, you're the cause you mustn't own, what takes shape as wonder now, and whenever each bottle comes with a proposition, youth's the corrosive wish.

Mundane and strange business

To bite down on a word
so you don't swallow
your tongue, your indignation's
the homeopathic remedy for yourself
you mist a mirror and
complain it's never clear
when you're near

To what extent is damage
the extrovert form of
transcendence, how long
before they came
to fear their non-white subjects
how has the historian managed to move
from thesis to truth
one group, in its quest for land they could
invent hymns for, forced
the other to scamper up the mountains
members sold into
wealthy households as playthings

To every weekend's task of painting over
graffiti, Never despair
being the easy moral, history
of little value, fragments of

igneous glass and rock
could only be repurposed as novelty
figurines, patriotic and cheap

To you and have you
observed the open
sea painted coffin
black, the spectacular sunsets
that inspired painters
to coin names for spectres
of pink, the deadly haze of the volcano
that birthed them, the brown boy
not chasing the women
they're the mysterious island
in his mind he's
just waiting for any saviour and

to put a warning on the flyer, the goal
is to not be reduced to entertainment
use a stage name if you're a stripper or
fortune teller, pickpocket or rat
if you've got money, train
the audience to heckle with accusations
like What for do old men moan like
young men in the night or What
is divorced from your language, debates
carrying silicate clouds across two oceans

To how wrong they were, shadows known
only by the imprints their bayonets make
for sons the best flexicuffs is obligation
sons forming alliances with native
women, each mestizo offspring gifted
three hectares of arable, sons
dressed like sailors, sons with
biceps and caps angled recklessly

to convey willingness
or conquest, whatever
they happen to be in
the mood for at 2 a.m.

Ode to boy

Boy's a murder of boys circling overhead, black feathers fluttering down the lens for effect, their appropriately creepy caws if pressed against your cheek cold or when boy rests his calves on your shoulders in indolence, rehearsed till perfected.

Or before boy, your true nature was something that could've come later, a point in the future unsure as a boy who intends to drop by but is deterred by another boy, the gate hasn't opened and when he barks the neighbours overhear the night.

You could've kept your true nature to yourself.

Because the age of revolutions is irretrievable as an orgasm, boy thanks you with the sweetest shrug, throws in a story about his unstable father. When it's your turn to share, boy butts in and spins a different trauma from a different parent.

Such a boy is hateful except when he's beautiful.

And Jesus, you'd have to look away after looking at him, and after he spares you a boy glance he's at once all the holes your hands have made, boy's the great flame that rises from your body, why's he so bright he casts no shadow.

Boy when he flies lands on your thigh and the wind his wings make is three-ply.

Get on it, it says, the sonnet about the crisis of self that gives you purpose when boy enters through a sliding door, beauty preceding him the way sunlight opens a hurt in your eyes, a pack of him surrounding you, boys howling at daytime. He wears a plum-blossom kimono and bares his torso at the slightest request.

When boy's too much, as he always is, there are other boys you could've always liked the best: the first boy, the third, fifth and sixth at the same time, ninth boy with bushy armpits, twelfth with research credentials, each boy its own particular charm and amulet. Especially delightful is the first week of every other boy, when mists so often shroud the otherwise universal sky:

while you've yet to wear the sky, boy's already its IG-worthy image.

Boy proves his tyranny by switching allegiances from week to week, which dragons must you slay, layers of rust on your armour, although his real talent lies in having the world on his side, like a jagged tooth of a boy who'll die young, and from a deck boy picks another queen.

Boy's the big mistake, as expected, but taking the stairs
on your way down, you feel your soul so gagged it's
no longer its own voice over. Boy when he swims
meets the crests, boy whose smirk you have to
shake off, boy

who fixes your quiff when he presses down, his body that's
acrid as wine in the forgiving night inspires mythic
ideas: boy's all Tadzio hair and bare feet, blue-and-
white striped cotton and thin-lipped amusement,
north star of a boy, boy with a reputation for virtue,
old boy who's lived to be too boy, frivolous boy,

mud boy who's begun to crumble, you're a pillar of salt,
knowing boy can only do you boy harm, your boy in
his boy voice tells you your boy future, inexorable,
while he holds a boy pillow over boy you, not uncruel
boy with potential, nothing's broken yet.

It's you who are. *What?*

A hummingbird.

To be old, to have
the body's laughter dislodged

in place of welcomed
glances, how is it
to be put up
with
thoughtless distaste or
undeserved respect, how is it

to inspire
nothing
is an adventure no
one's ever outfitted for and to
remind them of
their terror, the world

as it's deforming

yourself? Stop
the true disaster
is the first disaster.

The world uncontrollably slides into bizarre and grotesque derangement

The pale and secretive face is the future
carried through warm trees and unfamiliar rain. Thicket

that in a novel might have seemed exotic but in a war…
already self-heroic, miles from

the muddy road, check the ground for
snakes, smoke rationed cigarettes.

As if one were sixteen again, this one likes this one
this week, likes another the next, their invented triangles
a triumph of engineering.
Desire bids one
get past the point where to be kissed upon
parting is an impossible delight.

Boy with thorn, body a bronze abundance, hair

a Keatsian relic. Who, bending
over, opens up possibilities

like a wound. They overlook tallying the dead

of their enemy: against their four thousand, proof
you knew to grieve in private.

Why even keep track. One trades fish for wine
and their loyalty for favours nobody's eager to grant.

One grows bored borrowing a face
from another mirror. One just happens

to be just a person but
doesn't realise what this means, at what cost.

Softness and treachery
being what they have to make you you, your perfect mouth

its own form of violence
anaesthetises them from their virtues. They know most of all
their envy but conceal as best they can

the savage malevolence of their longing.

Every day one lives in themselves a generic hurt,
these islands have been sinking since they first knew
time, one hears they're of sand.

Because prosperity makes one an available target
they make no movement and rely
on shyness to give themselves character. One's heard of sand.

You inspire the tendency to accept injustice
if its end is beauty, are you your illness.
There is no end yet, only

its many monuments. Out of the white crosses
six thousand ghosts in olive drab rise to state, good little boys,

safe words. Hunger drives many to incoherence.

Nudged as if they were on open sea, one flees

inward and offers prayers. Rainwater collects
inside the well and to prop up each island, no more

than a boggy marsh, messy as sex, they drive wooden nails

into the water. One splits their palm
into flexion creases of half-truths.

What's told of you: grave
eyebrows, teeth so white they're blue, quick-loading Krag-Jørgensen,
dum-dum bullets, woman his white soul wakes into,

turning towards him, his fate yours,
you were beautiful, in your indifference
you were godlike.

There's barely any pain in winter

only obvious snow. There isn't a lot
of dirt so use one's hands. Say you're strange places

too tiring to cut across, say you believe
whatever you say about yourself—it isn't devilish

hard work—knowing so little of it.

No variations on time pressing

When he looks at a map of never to pinpoint the names,
there's no history

not worth plundering for poetry, when never hovers over
his mother's hometown like a slate cloud, there's a
stanza somewhere

there's his need to intercept the world, all the country's
terrors crushed

into simile. And never shapes it

according to the god he wants to kiss!!! the dire fate he
needs to miss!! every wandering mouth is recycled

bliss!

the bulldozed neighbourhood park he can't now ever
retreat to...

Aschenbach in crisis

This is the fiction someone else suffers a vaporetto.
Whisks him off the sandbar he tries escaping the fiction.
Where no one is ever eighty he knows he's a danger.
Of being aged out swamp and sea slip into his room.
The night before and warn him in a dream inside the fiction.

Leave they insist his body understands it into a sickness.
The body beyond wisdom drags its skin over another fiction.
Which is to remain the boat moves across the lagoon.
Past promise under the marble curve of the bridge the sea.
Is creased in colours but remains its ancient self even when.

His hunger makes the scum mean dread death orders.
Into a fiction the water littered with objects that people it.
Grocery bags and cigarette butts rats that tread and.
The face he peers over the starboard to see and fiction-like.
Explain but doesn't what in the morning arrives as half-regret.

A slight doubt about correctness gets jacked up into a hope.
He still thinks he could live in his feelings happen because.
There are real aches that mustn't be let in his joints.
Complain when he gets off the steamer he's back now.
To where he was you know that's how the fiction owns him.

Maliceless he returns to the same streets the morning winds.
Down for the summer island the little boy in him scampers.
Away his hunger scrounges for a fiction he could without care.
For safety devour the book heralds the end of his fiction is.
When he commits to you is a sentence of untrammelled welcome.

4

For the inability to wish for beneficial sobering is tantamount to dissoluteness.

As Aschenbach

It should've gone some other way, the man you still want to become a symptom of chance, afternoons infected by people's dissatisfactions, an undeserved tenderness for yours. Love's one window through which you enter middle age, and the diminishing future makes you sentimental, rote gestures turning into Through love stirs a night breeze or The way you part the curtains to let life in is a ceremony for him whom you can't disregard. It's winter where you are; he restores the odour of summer. Across the street snow on the roof glitters in shard-like threats, and these days abandon's greatest reward must be delay. Two hours before dark your version of a sun fizzes inside a stein and a ramekin of nuts lengthens with the evening. Life's a checklist of lonelinesses, but through him you think you are possible—yes, see sentimental. Go to the cinema alone, silk noose on, drape an arm over the next seat and think it the crucial instance of divine intervention. Step out for a smoke and breathe in the secret smell of his neck. Every wish is a mute wish, every mute answer's still an answer, and longing's the better routine. On the deep white of the parking lot a shadow that shimmies like wind. Look out, maybe this time every sign's a sign he's giving in.

Self-portraits with tyrannical consistency

Fig. 2. The man says the silence makes the bus a barge. You, lacking the compassion to leap past the literal, tell him it's because everybody else is sleeping, bone birches interrupting the cold white, sky a distracted blue. When you reach the house, he takes you down to the sauna in the basement. Yours for the moment is the kind of private life freed from most laws, you've yet to gain anything from this. Dry heat like the lame boy who can't walk fast enough to follow the doomed children into the river. The man guides him back home, tells him he's special now. You're now the one child who may or may not matter, depending on what you can do with your hands.

Fig. 4. The city has everything you would want to gawk at, except the relics of a great saint to call its own. An angel appears before the holy man you're named after and reveals the journey of his bones, centuries later two merchants travel to the next continent to fulfill the lore. Cranium and clavicle, sternum and sacrum, femur and fibula, they place the remains of his saintliness at the bottom of a basket, hide them with slabs of pork. The men fly back on a winged lion, the city swooning in ecstasy as it meets them, at which point you look at the man with a raised eyebrow, Where have you taken the punchline to.

Figs. 7 & 8. Ashen and hollow, the city loses its monuments in exchange for a richer history. No bombs, the man orders his army. But the enemy has never bothered to pick up his language, the university hall a gun nest, slabs falling off the façade. When the city finally goes quiet, the man walks around with a camera, lens trained on the artless insides of a civilian, the rubble that used to be a tenement, white soldiers drinking from a rusty artesian pump. You turn up the volume to hear the faint scratching noise beneath the voiceover. A woman leans against the one wall of her house and falls asleep.

Fig. 11. Citizens slip their ballots into the mouth of a stone god, his bug-eyed warning now nothing but an accidental feature of the city, the kind tourists easily overlook. Mossy flames shoot out of his brows, and the citizens orchestrate their fate based on who has the silverest tongue. The man spends his last few days in power watching their gifts of rosewater and balsam diminish. You see him walking along a corridor, his raiment the weight of a small child, he picks at a gold thread when you make small talk. They say he has everything but, because he wants more, they paint over his likeness with the heaviest black.

Fig. 15. The painting of the lives you covet is in the Museum of Quaint and Neglected Holidays, right next to a bánh mì store owned by a white guy and his tiny wife. The man you didn't come here with hugs you, which means Till we meet again is really a polite refusal. Nature, given over to random consolations, surrenders and delivers night and day, spring and autumn, death and death. And the man is a face glimpsed through the window as the bus pulls away, the man is sluggish smoke from the chimney. Look up, the man's a hazy moon, an amniotic hush whelms your evenings.

Fig. 19. Drab shore, sand the colour of the crook of your arm. The man teaches you curse words you pronounce clumsily, shows you a video of his hometown. Someone opens a bottle of room-temperature water, promptly freezing once exposed to the arctic air. When he says he feels smarter with you around, divine a future out of it. Understand that the way he brushes sand off your thigh is the answer to all the questions you need courage to ask. Back in the city now, walking to his flat for a quick fuck, he shouts at a vagrant huddled in a corner, there's nothing like heroism to turn you on.

Fig. 21. The man's voice takes you out to a pub, maybe the locals bark encouragements as you play pool, maybe the bartender's singing a song about Friday night. The man explains the game's origins, discusses its connection to horses at some point. You're on your sixth vodka tonic and all you can pay attention to is the slight curl of his bangs, the way his shirt sleeves ride up his arms. Cold is nothing to him. You've read the novel and decided to make it your life, strip it of the only thing that makes it interesting. The man is the boy, not as young but as inaccessible, and the unfortunate hero's one who, knowing distance is the cheapest conflict, says OK anyway.

Figs. 28, 29, 30. Mundane setting, made grandiose: evidence of the vision you claim to possess. How special you must be now that you're here and you. Describe the weather, ominous, to suggest impending loss. The man. Express unguarded admission as philosophical dilemma. You, embellished. Random fact, attempt to dispel the ponderousness. After two beats, let others in again so you could wear out your welcome. Tactical disclaimer: lament your myopia. Give in to that man, that man, and that man.

Fig. 31. The life proves impossible, he spends much of his in the frozen lake engraving bedtime stories on rocks. So you groom your own gills with a butterfly knife and half a bottle of whisky. You rest your throbbing neck on the hardened surface and from there try to see if any of the characters gets the reward you deserve. You can't read deeply enough, you're only the blue you can't know into. So the man comes up out of the water, records your anger with his phone, promises he won't ever delete it, skates over the obvious. Snow falls around your body like a contrivance, the mood cracking the discoloured ice with its heavy hands.

Fig. 34. Stuffed into a sack is a life you covet, slapping against the breakwater. They lay the sack on the pavement and untie its knot, the man crawling out, muttering apologies while tilting his head to let the bay out of his right ear. When he asks to borrow your phone, you stare at him with great fear, awe scratches at the hem of your pants. Panicked rat. The man has a face that can force forward the morning, street sweepers resuscitating the city's dignity. Minutes later a motorcycle pulls up, and the man slips the driver's face onto his head and drives off into the darkened yawn of a nameless alley.

Notes on terror

Tadzio of the glowing cheeks, tawny hair its own share of sky. Remember to keep to the late honey and early dirt.

Tadzio of the whitish sheen of sweat on the pontoon, half a second and it's vanished into the grain. Now when you know the legend and where in it you live, you touch the minutes, waver, and oil.

Tadzio of the gondola cushions, the warm evening blue as time shuffling across the garden, a bird you used to feed flying to its nest of spruce sticks and spit.

Tadzio of given mornings, white that assails from the open window, sunshine like mild rot. You listen to the waves, and slowly so, you're impure.

Tadzio of the browned feet and the coy hello. You rest your body on the sand and you're what the view has been missing all along, through you mourning finds its shape. Who owns the mouth that will honour it is the song every stranger knows.

Tadzio of the shoreline, pure boy in teal-and-white bathing suit playing tag with the shadows on the ground, you're on his left, you're his shock of joy. Take the train to one end of the borrowed city, and museums blur into regrets.

Tadzio of armpits smooth as a statue's, of shining knee hollows, of the amber universe, you're his youth sweeping out the last days and past. When you dig for the moon, you recoil in surprise.

Tadzio of the rust-coloured cabanas under which huddle the unmindful, the glinting blacks of his eyes never not on you. They share with you the weight of the petal and other deaths. Before you, Aschenbach did not like pleasure, oh

Tadzio, you're the tired gold of sunset, of ardour and unused heat, of horses drowning in the sea. There's tulle over the lampshade, tulle of the landscape, Tadzio. Mine, mine, the white word admonishes the world.

He had not expected this precious appearance, it came unhoped-for; he had not had time to settle his features into an expression of dignified calm

So you row the kayak with an efficiency that belies the loss of youth. Awe distracts you from your burning arms, your tinny voice describing the karst landscape as if it weren't obvious, the mossed-over cave mouth as it devours morning light. So you see less and less until there's only sound trickling down into more water, a local guide's rehearsed instructions. A god exists, who else architects this intricate dark, can erase you almost absolutely. You move from one version of terror to another, can you come back from it, of course you have, and he's beautiful to the point of remorse, as a gondola sliding across the night-infested sea works its placebo on the passengers, him touching his forehead to yours, as evening carries sleeplessly through riders in tandem and stray cats in heat, for every second he's still beautiful and you're this body's unstalwart excuse I'm the intruder who keeps rowing back out into the seen.

The servitude of normal routine gives way to the servitude of another's

1

When he speaks he speaks in a language that with a series of suffixes turns names of people, trees, feelings, weathers into their diminutives. The dead flower leaps back into its spring, the accident becomes a coastal town where guests laze away on the sand, the present a sarcastic aside, future a parable of impatience. In your birth language upon which you don't foist longings, every concession.

2

Boats are buried under snow and for months the lake exists only as collective memory. You don't pick up hair on the drain or sweep nail clippings off the floor so the hunger remains civil, you're not a stupid child who wanders into a forest where the requisite wolf hides, not the greedy animal too, the human inside you not praying to the god of normal mornings.

3

God of the crackling log, god of the cracked coffee cup, god of the soup spoon and fork with two bent tines, god of the three-hour sun, god of the manual left by the window, god of shorn-off thorns, like a god he refuses to grant mercy, after slipping on ice you laugh off your sprained wrist. God of the words he mutters in his sleep, god in the cigarette smell of the comforter,

4

god you can't not deny when he exists outside your half-truths, half the day's wholly yours. Until he wakes you don't take whisky with your eggs, as you're not your distress you don't rehearse your awkward bow unless urgent, though he snickers at your tramp and totter you're neither nor never. His hand pressing the small of your back is the same hand throwing a stick. Fetch, come back.

Ode to the exit sign

North star of the spunk-scented cinema, the fire before every fire, you're the ready come-on in the necessary dark. The nights have been hard and cold, but you're the one bright thing at this bar, the certainty of your command is aluminium. People hang out beyond you, passing around a pack of cigarettes, small talk flimsy as trust, sundry boredoms slapping each other's butts, rattling off cheap puns. O portal to the unlit alley where they dump vegetable peels, your authority is a nose that keeps spreading, your nose made of tiny scared men who pick up mugs and books made of more tiny scared men. Your body's a high-rise of tiny scared rank and file, you wrote once when in you was the same spirit that made you jump high enough to rip the exit sign off the ceiling. You didn't succeed but were endearing, your face in the white light of the hall so much older, a roughness absent in people your age, decay not yet inevitable, self-inflicted. No one sees your grey eyes through your glasses, I wipe the smudges off with my shirt, I twirl my shirt above my head to prove a point: everyone falls in love with you, you the LED party that inspires the great philosopher, your light smears his lips. I pray for my gorgeous skin, hypothetical skin, I wait for skin I deserve, want my decay to match yours, I've ached too long. Meanwhile I lie on the carpet as if I've eaten too much, flick my tongue as I spend hours knowing your face, you the Platonic ideal, everyone wants what you hide with your hands. I YouTube your name and every shy smile lives up to the truth of you, who deserve both epic and limerick. When everyone's shuffled out, you'll be the only thing on, unignorable as a threat, steadfast as a cockroach.

No truer variation on lives made independent of each other

Some years ! you come from outside ! ! frost sticking to your moustache ! ! fingers frozen ! ! and dedicate the evening to the maps and timetables I lay out on the table ! ! ! the trail of things things leave in their quick ! ! ! At the last moment ! you find relief in sleep ! ! and a fist cracks my dreams open ! ! ! Younger ! you feel your bones thaw while waiting for the bus to take you from the cemetery to your flat ! ! and I'm informed it's nothing but gas ! ! ! Straight away ! you want a bit of impromptu existence ! ! an exotic atmosphere with the occasional access to coke for the summer to be productive ! ! and since most days queer out-lustres class I parenthesise my grievances ! ! ! Once ! they bring you in ! ! a man with profitable habits takes you down a different path ! ! and I snap out of my reveries ! ! ! two gargoyles guarding the staircase ! ! ! In 1992 ! while you were new ! ! I draped a microfibre capelet over my shoulders and flew ! ! ! and now I know why you're too much with me ! ! ! Now awake at the hospital ! kimono-winged ! you ask for tea and garden air ! ! and like Wordsworth's god I'm transmogrified into the familiar outdoors ! ! ! After yet another tale of debauchery ! you renounce every kind of sympathy with the abyss ! ! and while I consider writing for children ! ! ! in the end I decide I want to be the synchronised gasps of all enviable fools instead ! ! ! Hopefully ! within your lifetime ! ! you would stand for courage or some other virtue that motivates despite catastrophe ! ! yours is always the brighter speech ! ! and you would see me at the far end of the hall ! ! ! stepping out with someone ! ! ! Weekends later ! in your books you discover a pre-epidemic hero-template that goes by different names but has your penchant for equivocation ! ! and I cash in ! ! ! my life like a window display ! ! ! sequined and holiday-themed ! ! ! As immediately as the morality brigade funds a campaign to penalise the trendiest amorous insurgence ! you whisper cynicisms as you sleep on the bus back to the capital ! ! and I replace injurious archetypes the way I open bottles ! ! ! with my teeth ! ! ! When the community puts up temporary shelters for the super-typhoon survivors ! what a no-good game it is to you ! ! how constantly defiance marks my days and how much denied satisfaction ! ! ! As soon as ! you walk into the room ! ! with your scruffy beard and crooked teeth ! ! I've already confessed you ! ! !

5

As if the charming psychagogue out there were smiling to him, beckoning to him. And, as he had done so often, he set out to follow him.

Ben Ben Ben Ben Ben

The narrator who foretold my life says passion is like crime
both welcome the weakening of society because they can profit off it

A month has passed in the novella and the locals are dying
as though thinking of you could make cholera a sunset backdrop

The barber who trims and darkens my beard says I've no fear of
    the disease
my personality plagiarised from my favourite characters, all magnetically
    staring out into the void

I think I'm alone because I manage romance
with a girlish evasiveness that's a front for sexual frigidity

When a man's already in front of me, too loose, the wanting slips off
my mind scrambles ahead to the ride home and Tim Tams before bed

I'm being facetious though not entirely incorrect
I pine for life-altering tenderness but prefer it in the abstract

Outside St Mark's I feed on impatience like the other pigeons
or like the sweet medicine death-smell of Venice I wait in ambush

More than wanting the reward I want to be the reward, the boy
who knows his beauty but not its magnitude, bending over a prie-dieu

I wish to be in a situation where I could say Am an attendant lord
though I'm pretentious I haven't gone beyond the required reading

The one denouement of all plotlines I repurpose for what you think of me is
in retaliation I write poems about impossible men with hairs on their backs

Sad Ben, sarcastic Ben, Ben who wakes at noon and pees while waiting for his tea to steep
and sighs loudly as he writes and microwaves burritos for brunch

You're Tadzio plus adult acne and the threat of a paunch and an open invitation to destroy me
though I won't die for you yet you're dreamt of the way he is

Your friends keep tagging you in pictures of smoky cafés, face turned away from the camera
I want to step into their bodies or be the thing you're looking away at

Ben of the macho sentences, Ben as bracing as a papercut, as permanent
Ben, you're mainly incontrovertible proof

Mann cultivated a public image of Teutonic reserve
among friends he was prone to nervous trembling and convulsive
    sobbing

Whenever nervous I replay in my head that scene in Clueless that
    references Monet
I use it as a conversation starter, it's one of the few insights I have
    into myself

I borrow Mann's biography from the library to discover why my
    impulses override my tact
when in his diary he draws a parallel between his sweet tooth and
    covert desires, he gets poetic

Extra fastidious he writes about his daily walks to the market to ogle
    shirtless workmen
in his fiction he defends himself when he writes about other people

All I want is to prove I orchestrate my life with the efficiency of a
    single mother
yeah that's another lie

I'm the videoke singer who licks the corners of their mouth between
    lyrics
I make every heartache ballad salacious, vaguely offensive, absurd

If in me are anxieties that need unpacking would you want to hear me
if not you then I want them exorcised with everyone's ear pressed
    against the door

The first time we shared a cigarette, just to connect you said
you preferred brawny men who could suffocate you, I looked at
    my hands

I congratulate myself for charming you into changing your
    preferences
never mind your girlfriend

The year you were born, overweight and swishy I had as much
    potential as a 349 bottle cap
I love you enough to look for confirmation in newspaper microfilms

Erap was the comic relief in the vice-presidential debates, needless
    to say he won
funny things stupid people say grabbed headlines 28 years ago, as
    they do now

A woman in her 20s was found stuffed inside a suitcase
she wore green basketball shorts, a cord around her neck, and
    a baby tee

Bakit Ako Mahihiya was showing at Ali Mall, not sure if it's a remake
    of the 1976 film
some days your beard's still scratching against my cheek, Ben

When I was born a man died from a cigarette he flicked at a bunch
    of balloons
do you know that a bunch of balloons is called a festival

I feel weird whenever your novel refers to a Southeast Asian
had to put it down when the Thai girl on the webcam plays with
    her nipple

At 16 I offered my married neighbour a blowjob
just because summer took too long and it seemed an important thing

You've gone over the age of Keats when he died
not enough time has passed for me to leave myself behind, fervently
    I giggle at your jokes

I've begun dating younger men, I'm embarrassed about it
I rely on Korean moisturisers to camouflage the fact

Before you're 30 your dishevelled pompadour will transition into
    a combover
Aged-out Asian Twink isn't a porn category, it's why I don't upload
    nudes to Grindr

Wouldn't you say we're perfect for each other
we deserve a maisonette in the suburb, we'd take turns vacuuming
    the carpet

You'd write your books and by 7:30 I'd set the table
for each other let's be someone's dreams, outside dailiness
    marooned forever

Love makes Aschenbach realise how much he neglected his looks
his intelligence made him assume beauty was an unnecessary capital

Translators differ on Aschenbach's lipstick shade
Appelbaum and Heim: raspberry, Luke: cherry, Lowe-Porter:
    strawberry

The point is he gets a horrible makeover, the kind you never see in
    romcoms
the point is it gives him enough hope to magnify the obligatory disaster

My role models are either abject homosexuals or doomed women
why don't you ask yourself what that reveals about you

Walking into a room I pretend my hand isn't mine and turn on the light
then recoil in dismay at my undisguised face, puzzle that one out

Aschenbach concludes his hope by eating lukewarm strawberries
he continues to stare longingly at the water before the epidemic
    bests him

Because hope has turned me into a bat inside a cave, I make
    screeching noises
still essentially alone though the acoustics are much better

The one time I asked about your girlfriend after your fourth lonkero
you said Sometimes you wake up next to a person and wonder why
    you're there

I've never experienced the luxury of being so bored you have no choice
    but to stick it out
this is a hint, Ben

Meanwhile I'm always dishonourable from a distance you won't bridge
poets can't soar upward, only commit extravagances, says Mann

And in the end hunger for a new naïveté, the severity of wanting only
    the feeling itself
for encouragement I curate a Spotify playlist of pathetic indies

When I run errands in Cubao everyone bops terribly to it as we do
    to fear
I want to keep sighing your name while I'm in the back of a Grab

Today I think about newly elected senators and keep all the doors
    locked
a man who's beside himself, says Mann, dreads becoming himself again

You've moved to Bulgaria, no longer sober you go drinking with the
    ballet dancers
are you finally single again, why haven't you declared your intentions

Just so Tadzio remains untouched by the epidemic and the
worshipper's fearful awe
Aschenbach considers telling the boy's mother to flee Venice

In Aschenbach's dreams his fear is a brutally insistent flute
when a heavenly VO shouts The foreign god, Mann drops a brick into
a beaker of water

In a field stands a gigantic wooden dick, worshipped by satyrs
this chapter-five dream is an orgy or a buffet or yet another unsubtle
contrivance

In my mind Gloucestershire is your neighbours climbing up the roofs
of their semi-detached
it's 2007 and being a teenager with drug issues you go back down for
your bass

But a three-foot flood's just another August afternoon to us
and by us naturally I don't include you

I pretend to be so used to horror I make off-colour jokes about it, that's
my ageing persona
like Mariah I contort my boxy body into sultry poses

I fold a frozen lake into my luggage before separately we leave
out of your lyric curtness I engineer elegiac caesuras, slightly lurid
and regretful

Smooth-skinned boys grabbing onto he-goats, Aschenbach's dreams
are Nick Joaquin dreams, the boys goad the goats

For Joaquin smooth skin isn't so much an indicator of youth as a given
hands tugging down my thermals, you already know this

Our post-coital talk would've covered random topics
the Hollywood starlet who honey-trapped the former president and
then survived

In the recording you could hear Marcos begging for a blowjob
reason gives way to violence, the headboard bangs against the wall

Dovie Beams wipes the saliva off her underboob, he asks if she
enjoyed it
no matter how white you are there's only one answer to a dictator

Eventually he tires of her and she wouldn't have it
she takes the tenderness in his letters and builds a press conference
out of it

In her final years she has a golden pool installed in her Beverly Hills
home
she dies free of him on the eve of Rizal's death anniversary

Mann says art is a war, a struggle people can't keep up for very long
I hope for the rest of my life to be as privileged

In Berlin you'd be the best person to keep drinking dinner with
you'd nurse a beer on the subway, I'd match your repartee

Everywhere cigarette butts wedged between cobblestones
I scuttle past streets that smell of piss and I'm flung to Manila with you,
    would this city do

I worry about the Philippine fishing boat rammed by a Chinese vessel
then get distracted by my hair collecting on the shower grate

I want to fly out to where you are, gallivant, order unpronounceable
    drinks
nothing but a backpack with underwear, mouthwash, your books as
    proofs of devotion

But as you know I'm a middle-middle-class citizen of a poor country
between you and me lie a hundred-dollar visa fee and a plane ticket

Spontaneity is a gift of the lucky
I have to retreat back into my low-cost longings

I show Jov a video of you singing Like a Virgin
I cover my mouth when he says The British have bad teeth, no

Sir Thomas Rich's School added a swimming pool in 1966
the potted history of your school says it was closed in the '80s but reopened in 1995

On Wikipedia's list of nationally significant events is a teenager who died
from drinking too much water while on Ecstasy, you were three and six months and 10 days

You got yourself a writing career at 17, fuck higher learning
at first I went straight to envy, now I wonder what it says about your inner life

You showed me your KS5 band covering The Pogues, thank god you outgrew that phase
instead you're always in a puffer jacket, through my window you can hear These Days

I enable my self-absorption, I'm silly enough to think it makes me interesting
I make obsequious bows, apologise to the world and my betters

I have to open another website to figure out what potted means
though I'm not dumb I don't know English

Aschenbach knows his last few days are his last days
the city government disposes of the sick, each one floating away like
 The Lady of Shalott

Professing love to someone who says it too easily is the second most
 exciting carnival ride
impertinent to stop a man who's about to jump into a river, says Wilde

I deal with chronic depression through pathological self-mythologising
or I sleep a lot, watch the same series until heart and soul I'm
 Kelly Kapoor

I don't ask but I wonder if you're still somewhat hot
if I press your jacket to my nose are you still your special odour

Wherever you are come back from the bottle shop, shake the snow off
 your boots
out of your stories I've built a house we wouldn't want out of

Don't you like editing your sentences until they're basically just verbs
I have so many verbs to give and so smash three plates, startle a cat
 for emphasis

I'm true as a Ponzi scheme and assembled from defence mechanisms
but let me be the most compelling version of myself with you

Love's a wheel rolling downhill, said a poet back when jeepneys were a
new invention
I especially enjoy fresh tread marks decorating my cheek

Mann offloads his gay shame onto his characters, makes the kyphotic
music lover kill himself
ambition was his antidote to self-disgust

I write long poems about shame, they're decent-sized flats
if enough people tell me how brave I've been I'd at least have use for it

I consider being funny but I only bring it out
when kindness, an offshoot of my need to be universally liked, proves
ineffective

Since I was 14 it's been my dream to be the person someone
masturbates to
at what age does transformation stop meaning various other
possibilities

What is the cure for shame, my shame indisputable as the mole on
my nose
I'm one of my lesser faces, Mann excised his by disfiguring Aschenbach

I check in on him, collapsing on the beach
and having depended on him for guidance, of course I end up thinking
Why not

After years of erotic austerity comes abandon, in Mann as in Freud
this means oblivion
punishment unretractable as academic tenure

Before it arrives Mann finally calls Aschenbach delusional
with Apollonian arrogance reasserting his moral ascendancy

And the world enters a new politeness, shame discarded like last millennium's plastics
like the unlicensed gondolier in chapter three, I try accepting disappearance

Ben, though I'm afraid of living as myself I don't want to be unafraid

Notes

All the poems contain passages from Thomas Mann's *Death in Venice*, translated by Stanley Appelbaum. The chapter epigraphs are direct quotations from the same novella.

The poems also draw from the following sources:

A documentary by Francesco da Mosto, another produced by the Smithsonian Channel; and a film directed by Luchino Visconti.

Various entries from *Encyclopaedia Britannica* and *New Catholic Encyclopedia*.

Exhibition notes from *Masters of modern art from the Hermitage* at the Art Gallery of New South Wales.

Fiction by Gregorio Brillantes; Ben Brooks; Italo Calvino, translated by William Weaver; John Cheever; William Faulkner; William Gass; Robert Musil, translated by Shaun Whiteside; and Raymond Queneau, translated by Barbara Wright; and the David Luke translation of *Death in Venice*.

News and feature articles by Gilbert Adair; Jenna Adrian-Diaz; Ted Aljibe; Tom Allard and Karen Lema; John L. Allen; Aurora Almendral; Mohammed Al-Mosaiwi; Kylie Atwood; Daniel Berehulak; Lian Buan; Regine Cabato; Helen Coffey; Hannah Ellis-Petersen; Patricia Evangelista; James Fallows;

Uki Goni and Jonathan Watts; Alissa Greenberg; Echo Huang and Isabelle Steger; Joyce Ilas; Lynda T. Jumilla; Kate Lamb and Ana P. Santos; Mario Alvaro Limos; Girlie Linao; Tats Manahan; Malou Mangahas and Karol Ilagan; Rey Panaligan; Pia Ranada; Edith Regalado; Miguel Paolo P. Reyes; Ana P. Santos; Elmor Santos; Amanda Shapiro; Rambo Talabong; and Jonathan Watts; as well as various articles from *Bulletin Today, Esquire Philippines,* and *The New York Times*.

The personal writings of Marcus Aurelius, translated by George Long; Ben Brooks; Hervé Guibert, translated by Christine Pichini; Ronald Hayman; John Keats; Joe Orton; Frederick William Rolfe (Baron Corvo); Sei Shõnagon, translated by Ivan Morris; John Steinbeck; and Teresa of Ávila, translated by J. M. Cohen; and the first-person accounts of Al Aronowitz, Danny Fields, Lou Reed, and LaMonte Young, via Legs McNeil and Gillian McCain; and Oscar Leuterio and Raymond Manalo, via Patricia Evangelista.

Plays by Yukio Mishima, translated by Donald Keene; Jean Racine, translated by John Cairncross; and Jean-Paul Sartre, translated by Stuart Gilbert.

Poetry by Mei-mei Berssenbrugge; Anne Carson; Richard Crashaw; Robert Creeley; Conchitina Cruz; Sor Juana Inés de la Cruz, translated by Michael Smith; Mabi David; Dalton Day; Emily Dickinson; Forrest Gander; J. Neil Garcia; Michael Grehsko; George Herbert; St. John of the Cross, translated by Gerald Brenan; Edmond Jabès, translated by Rosmarie Waldrop; Thomas James; Donald Justice; John

Keats; Rudyard Kipling; Federico García Lorca, translated by Sarah Arvio; W.S. Merwin; Fernando Pessoa, translated by Margaret Jull Costa; Ezra Pound, translated into Finnish by Tuomas Anhava, and retranslated into English via Google Translate; Lisa Robertson; Jaime Sáenz, translated by Forrest Gander; James Schuyler; Anne Sexton; Ron Silliman; Jack Spicer; José Garcia Villa; and Elizabeth Willis; and a translation of *Kalevala* by John Martin Crawford.

The scholarly, philosophical, and polemical writings of Louis Althusser, translated by Ben Brewster; Mikhail Bakunin, translated by Sam Dolgof; Oscar V. Campomanes; Steven Edwards; Vilém Flusser, translated by Anthony Mathews; Michel Foucault, translated by Lysa Hochroth and John Johnston; Louise Glück; Paul Guyer; Angela Jones; Andrew Lang; John A. Larkin; Primitivo Mijares; Pankaj Mishra; Linda A. Newson; Friedrich Nietzsche, translated by Anthony M. Ludovici; Massimo Pigliucci; Raymond Plant; Peter I. Rose; Friedrich Schiller, translated by William F. Wertz, Jr.; and Peter N. Stearns.

Song lyrics by Angel Aponte, Dwayne Carter, Kendrick Duckworth, and Miguel Antonio Rodriguez Diaz; Daniel Bejar; Shawn Colvin; Nadir Khayat and Stefani Germanotta; Stevie Nicks; Lou Reed; Andy Thompson, Lazerbeak, Chance Lewis, and Dessa; Ann Wilson, Nancy Lamoureaux Wilson, Holly Knight, and Walter Block; and Rick Wright.

A webpage maintained by the UNESCO World Heritage Centre.

Acknowledgements

Special thanks to the editors of the following publications for including these poems, often in earlier versions: *Bœst* for 'As Aschenbach' (There's no knowing now), 'Aschenbach in crisis,' and 'Notes on terror'; *Bent Street* for 'Ben Ben Ben Ben Ben'; Electric Literature's *The Commuter* for 'Ode to boy'; *Foglifter* for 'Motus animi continuus'; *Headway Quarterly* for 'As Aschenbach' (Who setting out to voyage); *Heights* for 'He had not expected this precious appearance, it came unhoped-for; he had not had time to settle his features into an expression of dignified calm' and 'Motus animi continuus'; *Kritika Kultura* for 'As Aschenbach' (This isn't about how), 'Variations on the word "pass,"' 'Wind and teeth,' and 'Wonders and terrors of the variegated earth'; *Mascara Literary Review* for 'One among'; *NightBlock* for 'He was most surprisingly conscious of an odd expansion within himself, a kind of roving unrest, a youthfully ardent desire for faraway places, a feeling so intense, so new or at least unaccustomed and forgotten for so long, that he stopped short as if rooted to the spot'; *Pinwheel* for 'Essays on transformation'; *Social Alternatives* for 'No longer was he young and raw though the error remained young and raw' and 'It's you who are. *What?* / A hummingbird.'; *Sporklet* for 'The servitude of normal routine gives way to the servitude of another's'; *The Hunger* for 'Naïve and sentimental' (Back when he rode shotgun); *The Night Heron Barks* for 'As Aschenbach' (It should've gone some other way); *The Spectacle* for 'Ode to the exit sign,' 'Self-portraits with tyrannical consistency,' and 'The world uncontrollably slides into bizarre and grotesque derangement'; and *Yes Poetry* for 'Ben Ben Ben Ben Ben.'

This book exists because of an assortment of kindnesses.

Deeply indebted to Lisa Gorton for patiently going through various drafts and for the inspiring edits. For the time they devoted to the manuscript, so much gratitude to Martin Villanueva, Michael Balili, Christian Jil Benitez, Raphael Coronel, and Raymond de Borja.

Thanks to the University of Adelaide for giving me the space and resources to write poetry again and in earnest. Especially grateful to my supervisors Jill Jones—whose guidance throughout the drafting process allowed me to consider this sequence from various angles—and to Aidan Coleman and Brian Castro. Thanks to the D R Stranks Travelling Scholarship and The Walter and Dorothy Duncan Trust. Thought about and realised a number of the poems in this book at the residencies granted by the Civitella Ranieri Foundation and Villa Sarkia: thank you for the support.

For the gift of their company, thank you to Jov Almero, Nica Bengzon, Francheska Berdin, Rogelio Braga, Oscar Campomanes, Daniel Carreon, Ember Corpuz, Rodrigo Dela Peña, Jr., Glenn Diaz, Austere Rex Gamao, Christian Genova, Vito Hernandez, BBP Hosmillo, Raees Khan, Jiuhn Kim, Frank Liao, Paolo Manalo, Kay Marie Martinez, Marty Nevada, Jeremaiah Opiniano, Elaiza Lanozo Orlino, Michael Rey Orlino, Trevor Pook, John Lorenz Poquiz, Carlos Quijon Jr., Stephen Redillas, Bernice Roldan, Vincenz Serrano,

RJ Taduran, Mehbuba Tune Uzra, Maria Amparo Warren, and Jasmine Watson. Thank you to Jennefer Lyn Bagaporo and Rio Maligalig for preparing some of the best meals I've ever had in Adelaide, and to Leandro Sakamoto and Livia Sakamoto for taking me with them to Phong Nha, where some of the poems are set.

To LA Dacula, Marlon Lacsamana, Denise O'Hara, and Rhoda Mae Tanyag: for never not understanding. And as always, all my love to my beautiful family: Emma and Cecil, Nanay Zon, and Maecel and Corsie.

This book is for Janice O'Hara: it was from her and Denise's bookshelf that I first picked up a copy of *Death in Venice*; this obsession is their fault.

About the author

Mark Anthony Cayanan is a poet from Angeles City, Philippines. They obtained an MFA from the University of Wisconsin in Madison and are a PhD candidate at the University of Adelaide. Their poetry books include *Narcissus* (2011) and *Except you enthrall me* (2013). Poems from this book have appeared in, among other journals, Electric Literature's *The Commuter, Kritika Kultura, Mascara Literary Review, Sporklet,* and *The Spectacle*. A recipient of fellowships to Civitella and Villa Sarkia, they teach literature and creative writing at the Ateneo de Manila University.